HOUSEFIRE ELEGIES

HOUSEFIRE ELEGIES

KEITH MONTESANO

Gold Wake

Contents

Two

For Jess and Maya

ONE

COME HOME TO ME

After the kiss on my cheek each morning,
        I haven't told you how I can't fall asleep
                when it's over—always some problem

with my imagination. *Come home to me.*
        It could be the woman who has a stroke
                in the middle of her craniotomy,

her left hand shooting up to wrench
        your neck, your footing lost, back
                of your head slammed against the cold floor.

Come home to me. The construction constant
        around our city: operator drunk, you singing
                God-awful music from a disc I burned you

earlier, excavator's claw bound to smash
        the windshield, sweep across your body.
                Too many movies, and more being made,

of lost love, old men regretting their lives
        of mistreatment and alcohol abuse. Always
                those components. Always an ending

with no redemption. *Come home to me.*
        And our scene in a liquor store: fingers
                tapping wine bottles before his ski mask

and bat in hand. My nightmare in this world
        is bound to happen. I rush him, scream
                for you to run. The last thing I see is the back

of your head, slow-motion curls bouncing
        for one utopian second—*Come home to me*—
                before the bat cracks my skull.

CITY'S EDGE

When the sky opens, raining money instead of blood,
        you can ask for more favors: baskets and nets for all, free love

without its impermanence, the rushed construction of bridges

        before collapse—anything so that in your hand the gun
now of no use begins to grow cold, unfamiliar, some kind of gift

        used years ago, when needed, when life's blank pages

were left for dead, soaked with storm and understated
        longing. Our city has asked that we show our affection

with confetti and streamers, naked streaking over ruined trellises

        which are now silent homes for black widows
and their millions of tiny spawn. These days are like egg sacks

        exploding, only silent, all of us to die in the unwritten fire,

history unearthed years from now, with nothing left but an offering
        of this dissipated past. When we sleep, the red sky

always shrouds, framing impossible maps on our skin, splaying

        buckshot droplets like halted rain, spherical crosshairs
over everything like brushstrokes we'll always leave behind.

        But what painter's hand has lost control, plans to mark us

permanently with the darkest colors of this night? We could ask
        just one thing, we're told, and that is all. We imagine ourselves

at this highest point: lights blinking out below, cars sputtering

        in the cold dark toward destinations unknown by their drivers.
We wanted to be that way once—on top of that hill, near the edge—

        looking down at nothing in our hands but each other's.

VARIATION ON A LANDSCAPE

After Joel Sternfeld's Photograph,
McLean, Virginia, December, 1978

Former horror-film house in the background:
    photographed before scrapped in nearby landfills.
        What was contained within windows and boards,

the frames buckling, asbestos even withered
    in such heat? Always some hand turning black,
        pressed to window glass for seconds before

retreat, as dying trees mask firemen—hidden
    and frozen in the decay—shooting water toward
        the flames, dousing the roof with anything to stop

the burning. And the market, positioned so close
    to one fireman as he chooses the best pumpkin
        wonders if he'll later jam needles into its skin

before they pierce the boy who tries to grasp it,
    unable to escape with his palms gushing blood.
        Always some scythe sweeping wheat nearby,

onlooker spotting grey smoke, too far away
    to glimpse the flames, the slowly mechanizing crane
        raising and lowering the hose as dusk turns

its darker blue, hovers around the lone pine,
    maples bare and vanishing, their leaves already
        seeping into the ground. How far did they come?

And what was worth saving? Sometimes I hope to drive
    for weeks until I find that house. But thirty years later,
        what's left is blood and bone, hair growing

under the graves, the frame leveled, its charred excuse
    now an empty lot and strip mall. I want to ask them all
        why they didn't help. *Someone started the blaze,*

dropped a lit cigarette, knees locked from a heart attack, fell asleep
by a candle under the ceiling fan. Someone probably burned
among such beauty. And this could be anywhere

of all the places I have lived. Because everything feigns
brightness before it turns black, and as night finally fades,
we'll always trap ourselves within these walls.

WISHING FOR A NOCTURNE INSTEAD OF AN ELEGY

None of us were supposed to see it—every passenger
    in the same direction, sipping coffee, turning dials
        on the radio—but all of us saw it, near dusk, the man

nearly chopped in half by the red Chrysler
    on the Jefferson Davis, how everything that happens
        in that moment is your only and entire life.

I don't think I made a sound. In the cold, my windows
    were closed, the heat spiraling inside, breaking lattices
        of crusted grey snow on the windshield—

clean of spider cracks and broken glass, flecked blood,
    his entwining limbs. But I saw him look both ways,
        intentionally, as if the accident were truly an accident.

The sky was sick with gaseous pinks, and we were all
    just minutes away from post-dusk drunkenness.
        As it was we didn't stop. I looked in my rearview

after one ragdoll bounce, saw a few cars avoiding him,
    and after trying to forget, turned onto my street.
        Moments later I would have seen nothing.

Delay: Dulles International Airport

Just one day ago my niece was born while 29 coal miners

      were killed in the Upper Big Branch mine explosion

in West Virginia, and as I sit staring at planes that will never

      leave the ground, headphones on, I wonder if Bruce Hornsby

really knew life in mining towns: *Watching out...as it all goes up*

      in flames. Out of fifty on-time flights, the only one delayed

is ours: ten passengers who wait, half-asleep, as night turns to morning,

      the black sky starless, unchanging. When I do get home,

four hours late, you'll be working on a craniotomy, a man

      who crashed his motorcycle into the back of a semi, lanes stalled

for miles on Route 17. *Fire, smoke-filled lungs*, he sings, and I can't

      imagine such collapse, weight too much for limbs

and blood flow. The airport bar closed hours ago. The lights of all

      terminals are dimmed, and six ladders still surround

our plane: front compartments opened, colored wires crossed

      and re-crossed, screwdrivers twisting, all to get us off the ground.

But nothing seems to work as hours still pass, and almost everyone

      is sleeping by now. I keep looking at your text, *He won't make it*,

as my eyes close, and my niece howls her way into the world.

WHAT FOLLOWS

At two in the morning, there's the constant growl
of the turbine air conditioner of the North Shepherd

apartment complex, that roof where I've watched
couples make love beneath the glowing stars

of Richmond, bruised lights flickering from cop cars,
precoital drunks flanking sidewalks, wavering

in side street alleys: a friend holding up another,
pulling hair back so night's evidence won't stain

her clothes. At 2:06 a scream echoes down a corridor,
and a woman's muffled voice follows: *Call the cops*

and stay inside, before the screen door slams on the porch
of the corner house across our street. I try to think

like a witness, but time here doesn't matter now.
What did it sound like? A gloved hand wrapped

in latex over a mouth. Or something beautiful:
a string quartet at a wine bar. Concentrated drunkenness

fusing with dusk. I could say it's twenty after the hour
when I hear the sirens, could ask why a little girl

was out that late, but that continuous shrill
of summer's breath eclipsing everything

drowns out all the voices: every witness and headline,
passersby hoping to catch a glimpse.

Snowstorm and Power Outage

Already, panic has begun. And questions: Who will crash? What
will burn instead of generators flaring, transformers exploding—

shriveled power disintegrating into the air—lightning surging
into gunmetal bursts? I want so badly now to hold you under this sky,
but already you're asleep as lights pop on and off in massive dilation,

snow rattling our windows. We hear fire trucks and minor collisions
at the end of an alley. Our power wavers: *Car into a telephone pole?*

Dying tree limbs collapsing power lines? We've never seen Richmond
like this: where wars weren't reenacted, where horses trampled
through grass before street grids, unlike Pennsylvania, where school

was never canceled, where we drove drunk after last call, roads
never too slick for us to handle. There are few cars now, three floors

below, wheels spinning as they turn from street to street. I'm sure
we're not the only onlookers, but no one else can be seen.
You asked me the other day how we ended up here, or maybe how

you ended up here, and I took the *How* to mean *Why*. I imagine
unmonitored fireplaces, roofs weighted to collapse, hidden sparks

waiting to catch anything that will burn. But we're safe now, we think,
and consider ourselves the smart ones, not out swerving over roads:
necessary drives toward dying fathers, perpetual business trips,

addicts shuddering through alleys to find warmth in their veins.
I have candles burning, our flashlight crank-turned and shining.

There are those assuming this will be the end, feverishly kissing
as only six inches come down, and for the moment, I want to be
next to them as the snow changes to hail. On the other side

of the country, Californians flee from wildfires, and the fifty
who died months ago in the Buffalo plane crash may look down

upon us now, unable to lend forgiveness. Tomorrow we'll hear
of fuel trucks separating on the interstate, splitting slowly as the hail
turns to rain, to black ice, its chaotic invisibility. The lightning rips

like distant, seconds-long bombs, and while no one reaches
fire escapes, some have packed and, for now, left this world behind

while others take let's-make-love-before-we-die as the only thing
they have left. You may be asleep right now, but without the fan whirring
its white noise, the silence will keep me awake all night, as one

streetlight still flickers in blackness while children, with school
canceled for days, remain tucked in their beds. What we want

is to say we feel something: the this-may-be-it that we live through,
the ton of metal beneath us when flat tires skid our families
toward guardrails. And in this city of grids and apartments and always-

just-miles-away shootings, we're locked into something now, something
we tell ourselves will not end in ash, drifting down to blanket us all.

NEXT ROOM

Last night, only ten blocks
        from where we slept,
                a police chase before

the destined crash jarred
        sleeping families awake,
                the accordion-coiled metal

from each car landing
        upturned on cross-street
                sidewalks. And when I say *we*,

I mean *you*—always awake
        I seem these days, predicting
                steel-toes kicking in our doors,

cats below us knocking
        space heaters into curtains,
                the building's sleep too deep

to awaken from the fire.
        It's as if the cold, depriving
                moisture from our skin,

forebodes our future withering,
        the sirens and their spinning
                mirrors cracking and exploding

under the weight of it all.
        Now, on the balcony listening,
                I ask: *How many blocks away?*

How many involved? Has anyone
        been saved? And as I wait
                for sleep, hear you breathing

in the next room at dawn,
        I'm afraid the sky won't change,
                endlessly echoing this night.

THROUGH THE CITIES AS WE MOVE
CLOSER TO OUR WEDDING

Nothing could help me from stopping
by every single rail yard we passed

along the way, wondering who might
be sleeping there in the distant dusk:

teenagers among parents who wouldn't share
their blessing, addicts squinting their eyes

to God, or those strung out and rejected
by the mission, all wishing they had a few dollars

to share stories in the nearest bar, cold beer
a pitiful excuse for healing. We drove hours

that day—through towns in Virginia we didn't know,
wineries around every turn, mansions

on every hill—before the semi followed
too closely, almost running us off the road.

At every stoplight: boarded shops
and For Sale signs, weeds choking tracks,

our love I hoped would last until one of us,
grey light seeping down on our faces,

regretted everything. I wanted to stop, walk through
streets we'd never name, root through

rat-infested warehouses, breathe in the rot
of every single city, for all the cities, my love,

are turning in on themselves. And it's just a matter
of time until the deer emerge from the woods—

clouds blackened overhead, fences lining yards
along these roads like miles-long snakes—

to calm our nerves, if only for a moment,
before everything ends.

VARIATION ON A LANDSCAPE

After Amy Stein's Photograph, *Route 14, New Mexico*

All these urban legends: helping someone stranded before
        you're stuffed into a trunk,
the accommodating man with a hook for a hand

        after serving in Vietnam,
the priest hit by a drunk driver somewhere on Route 80.
        Or my own head bashed

over and over on my windshield when I was 16, neck
        almost snapped, choked
for what seemed like an hour on Mehard Road. No one woke

        with some sense of dread.
No one predicted danger across manicured lawns. Always
        the coma lasting too long,

the saddest stories heard in passing. Why help someone
        in a city you don't know,
much less the ones you do? What can we make out: headlights

        glowing like a town
of prairie dogs, spanning miles, glaring through dense fog.
        Above them: silhouettes

of both passengers, open hood looming like a headline,
        somewhere along blank
desert stretches I may never see again. *I will die on a road*

        in New Mexico—a capable
driver, eyes off the road, reaching for a cigarette—
        on a day I can already remember.

OPEN WINDOWS

What I felt bad about wasn't the girl
stabbed and left for dead, but thinking

it may have been you—the girl I dated
for three years in high school—coughing

in some damp alley, an air conditioner
hanging from the window above,

dripping its rhythmic condensation
outside the now boarded-up bar

as 2 a.m. drunks shuffled by, wondering
if they could remain anonymous, if anyone

would call for help. But it was the girl
who pulled the same stunt I did

when I was 14: chugging vodka
in the woods between halves at a high school

football game. I had no doubt
it was you, when I thought I was in love

those years ago: early morning
drives through silent roads, books consumed

at home until sunrise, sleep
a thing of the past. Months ago

a girl was found hanging near an oil derrick
a few towns from ours, her book bag strap

coiling the power lines after she climbed
those twisted metal pegs

to the top. What did the boy who was blamed
think after hearing this? Now, I'm thankful

it didn't happen to you. This is no
test of my ego or some excuse:

everything could've been my fault then.
And as Jess lies asleep now—open windows

inviting drunken screams, wailing sirens,
transient addicts rattling rusted shopping carts

through brick alleys below our apartment—
I hope I never think of you again.

LAST PAGE:
U.S. AIRWAYS SAFETY INFORMATION CARD

Everything calm: emergency doors opened, bright yellow
      inflatable slide perfectly filled with air as the passengers
slide down, excitement on their faces as they think not of their lovers
      untroubled because they have no idea, their children
charting Magellan's paths with bright crayons at school, and even
      the neighbors, unaware they'll never see them cutting grass
or sipping beer on the porch ever again. The last page, finally:
      the one where the plane might land in the Pacific, Atlantic,
or some small lake in some smaller town, where chances
      are less and less for survival. Do their eyes show infinite
sleep, that this is already some purgatorial existence? Again
      the calmness: the reach below the seat, mind running through
silent charades of the flight attendant, with all the time in the world.
      The last four panels: a father securing a lifejacket
over his daughter's shoulders, chanting over and over: *We'll be fine.*

SIRENS AND WILDFIRE

All through this night, rain prepares to drown our bodies,
          render us
speechless. But who needs words with squad car squall

          and fire trucks
racing through magic hour, stray dogs searching for scraps
          left in cans,

palms pressed to every living room window? Love, our days
          are shortened
with each breath. California, in pixilated smoke and film, is in flames,

          will remain
a tree stump charred to kill the fire ants. We'll travel there eventually,
          to a landmark

not in bronze, but the blackened silhouettes of our lives. Sirens,
          please help us.
A murderer's kicking in my door. The neighbors are screwing

          like rabbits—
their webcam streaming—hoping to leave something behind
          that's beautiful

and ravenous. Wildfire, sing your songs to end us. The ice is melting
          and we're all
falling through, cold enough to gasp but unable to speak, frozen

          before the moment
we ask ourselves why everything's blurred under water, why
          the helicopter has no sound,

the rope ladder not uncoiling, search lights dimming as we hope
          we'll turn to bronze
like the statues on Monument Avenue: swords unsheathed, crows

          perched on our shoulders
where moonlight falls like sheets, diaphanous shrouds,
          until the final Siren calls.

Beginning with the Fear of Drowning

Amelia Island, Florida

To the left and right of our balcony, parts of each wing
at the Ritz-Carlton are getting work done: cream-colored sheaths
shroud the scaffolding, ten floors high, the height

the worker fell from nearly four months ago
at Binghamton University. Past the brash Spanish of the crew,
just thirty yards from my vantage point, past the cascading grind

of drills, echoing trill of pipes from hammers, the ocean lends
its false calm through the din, the perfect-lined horizon in the distance.
Somewhere, in some ballroom below, you're listening

to the keynote speakers and doctors go on
about their findings, starting with the list of stroke signs.
What I know is sometimes half the body loses gravity

and the mouth turns to clay. Your Mayo Clinic flash drive,
left on the white sheets, tells us more than these words can
about depression cures, muscle therapy, confidence

for entering the real world again. A few days ago a student
at Rutgers committed suicide after his roommate recorded him
fucking another man. It's awful to put it like that, I know,

but it's why I can't even think of having children now:
the too-much they see too young, unable to grow
as adults before flailing themselves into the Hudson

from the George Washington Bridge. Now, looking out
beyond the sno cone blue umbrellas lining the beach,
I wonder if the end of *Interiors* could truly happen: a destined

walk into the ocean, the rip current taking Eve, if she thrashed,
coughed, too devoid of human thoughts for the mouth to fight back
through speech, the garbled rasp of her last fighting breath.

WATCHING THE LIVE FORT HOOD MEMORIAL
AT ASPEN DENTAL

Among the poorly hung TV, the drab pastels and wrapped gauze
 inside our mouths, all of us watch: boots strung together
on each pedestal, horns playing as "Taps" disintegrates into memory
 while backgrounds and collective thoughts dissipate like hums
of drills and machines finally clicking off down the halls. I have never
 fired a real gun but plugged seven white rabbits with pellets
and blew heads off robins near the birdfeeder years ago, tied legs
 and flung each mass into the woods beyond the birch trees.
I've been here an hour. The waiting room reeks of unwashed hair
 and unbathed children while the cold, unrelenting, attacks skin,
the spreading, splotched red of my face. I know when it gets worse
 they'll stare even more, wide-eyed kids sucking crayons
and fingers, unblinking. But I had fluoride when I was young, a mother
 who chose sugarless gum and still can picture Wade Whitehouse
in *Affliction*, finally wrenching his tooth out with pliers, all of us
 surrounded by teeth, X-rays of cavities and inflamed gums,
of gleaming white. There's beauty in the commercial of the bullet
 entering a glass bottle's lip before it shatters the bottom
like a thousand stars, unlike the round through our teeth—fragments
 we hope identify us someday—undaunted by the care we took.

Variation on a Landscape

After Stephen Shore's Photograph, *Bay Movie House,*
Second Street, Ashland, Wisconsin, July 9, 1973

Without the cars in front, this could be anywhere
        in any town, even miles from where we live now,

dusk looming above the marquee, every actor alive then—
        Buttons, McDowall, Albertson, O'Connell—

with the others, deemed minor, who never had
        careers like those we know today. A star or dust speck

or sliver of moon: something catches the eye
        above glowing neon red and blue. I think of my parents—

a year before my brother was born, a year before
        family was the only priority—buying two tickets, less

than two dollars for a matinee, I not yet born,
        when couples went home after the credits, not thinking—

like I did when I first saw it—that Belle Rosen would never
        come up for air, that their breath would be held forever.

Honeymoon Meditation: Flight Number 1967

Never able to sleep on planes, this is no different: too many
passengers, sun gleaming into windows while children,
seatbelts unbuckled, play action-figure-killing-action-figure

as the flight attendants tell them every few minutes
to remain seated. Of the many crashes this year,
what goes through their minds? To see every continent

and city, even for a glimpse, and to name what most
see only in photos, to finally go down unlovingly
into oceans they've slept above countless times

over the years? Next to me you're sleeping, open-mouthed,
turning and twisting every few minutes, never finding
a comfortable position. Only the pilot knows where we are,

and for that our thoughts are masked by trust as we assume
we'll land perfectly, with only minor turbulence along the way.
I want to ask the flight attendants to describe their fears:

Are you frightened every time the wheels lift off the ground?
Do you worry your husband's having affairs? Don't you know
this is how you're going to die? There's something beautiful

about every one of them, something I can never explain.
Next to me, your eyes still closed, facing the window, I can't
tell you what I'm dreaming: our bodies lulled, then sinking.

TO THE MUSES

The Florida weather was balmy, and you imagined
        the three girls leapt from the bridge like Olympians,
curled into something beautiful from a train turning,
        slow-motion, into crushed steel, a million wheels
squealing. We want to believe *More Love* spray-painted
        on the rusted bridge is something God wrote
that each girl would have a chance to experience
        everything in her future. The news shows a boy,
a survivor, running his hands through his blond hair,
        tears about to start before he turns from the camera
zooming in on his face. The man interviewed says
        he will never sleep again, imagines sparks catching gasoline,
a train car erupting in flame, drinks tossed, windows
        busted, everyone escaping into water below the bridge.
And that would be it: the story we hope to hear,
        cheating death, nature, or attempted murder. The man
says he will never sleep again. The sound of the wheels
        like a child screaming directly into his ears.

WHAT THIS MEANS

The many shots of crane and ascension, cars piled up,
        the birth of flowers, split stems, roots pushing
    through soil, all the bloom and glimmer, the hope

    that the collective can come to a decision as this
will be their opening. What they imagine, finally,
        is a low-angle camera right behind the heels—

shoes caked and sinking—as they splash wet mud
        into the lens, all of it sticking, with distant clouds
    in the azure-morning sky, a warm day in the midst

    of winter, something an audience can't believe is real,
but buys it and sits on the edge of gnarled seats
        in the theater. What's real is how, dear reader, only

I can imagine it: how he never puts on the hazards,
        a car swerving right, an elongated squeal of tires,
    unenhanced as he opens the door, takes off, music

    something cacophonous like Coltrane's "The Father
and the Son and the Holy Ghost," dual saxophones,
        staccato brushes on snare and crash, and you

can tell me that's a beautiful piece of music—
        something I'll never see because beauty,
    now, is far between the moments we almost

    never have, and yet how can that title not lead us
to beauty? Dear reader, I'm done with speculation
        because I have the truth, or what I imagine it to be,

from the woman I love. When they found her
        you tried to save her. Every attempt is easy.
    But what I don't know is the name of each part

    of the brain, something I could look up, names
I could write in ink that would convey some true
        sense of music, curled tongue in the mouth, lack

of pronunciation, the robotic, mechanical voice
                    speaking: *occipital lobe* as if I'm supposed to know
          the functions, how one slight push can move

          muscles, nerves, the lips before they became clay,
the immovable counterpart to destroyed love—
                    from black ice, from the awful weather in this place.

You told me that her brain—when the doors
                    burst open, when you couldn't tell me that a skull
          sometimes busts, unable to protect what

          we were born with—was coming out. *Coming out.*
And what can we do then? But it wasn't us.
                    It was her husband, who almost died as he sloughed

through snow and mud and grass and earth
                    to get to her, who heard a high-pitched ringing
          in his ears like a bomb went off and kept running

          and finally got to the car and tried to hold her
in his arms. He meant to keep driving, but he recognized
                    her car. What I can't tell you is they were on their way

together. What I can't tell you is that he recognized her car.
                    What I can't tell you is what he felt when he held her
          in his arms. Cars passed. I can't believe I've left you here.

Last Words

Smoke from the pipes of our lungs, unreaching, shifting molecules
        to air and back
to smoke, will leave us in the midst of this city quietly to drown

        among our past—
suicide gun blasts through walls, our waiting and heart-stopped nerves
        then quickening,

then beginning their stretch like windswept ash, grey spores floating
        until they're trapped
within the bricks. I've waited too long to call the police or 911,

        and yes, always
some regret remains. There was the chorus of cop cars before my own
        slowed to a red light,

before a speeding SUV would've ripped off my head, cleanly, leaving it
        to stare back
at my body in some other dimension with ghostly wonder.

        When voyeured
park-bench homicides seemed to follow me, I felt the blood
        and thought how

I loved you even more, hoped if you were a block behind me
        you'd soon stain
your hair with it, chalk-mark my body red instead of white, so rain

        could wash it off,
pool it into sidewalks where we'll be after conflagration and a sky
        lit to the first stroke

of dawn: not rosy-fingered, but the blue flash before the body burns,
        before the skin turns
to bone, when we'll never know how or who we loved before.

DEAR SICKNESS

Thomas Mortimer IV Left Note at Crime Scene...

Before Thomas Mortimer stabs and bludgeons
      his sleeping family, we watch *Saw*, *Irreversible*, *Traces*
            of Death—a concocted horror trilogy back-to-back—

effects magic and makeup, poorly lit scenes,
      delayed head-splits and body-sized gunshot gashes.
          And we stare, rewind, stuff popcorn

into our mouths before cautiously nearing the end
      of the bag, knowing our enamel gets weaker every day
         that one thick kernel can split a molar, strike its nerve.

My dream lately has been of myself as a boy
      in my father's car, stopped to help Mortimer's
         white jeep, staring at the jack inching up the frame,

my father twisting the lug wrench, fingers tapping
      as Mortimer watches, wonders if my father recognizes
         his face, the license plate. I keep looking—face pressed

against backseat glass, breath fogging—wiping away
      to see him tighten the last. The nightmare ends with you,
         his daughter—as he covers her eyes before the slice

with a kitchen knife—and luckily those, your eyes,
      are masked while you sleep now, blurring into his daughter
         by the end, with my eyes, a boy's eyes, imagining

you already gone, the white jeep before we drive off,
      my father saying nothing. And right before I wake,
         I pray that the white light ahead won't burn us alive.

SLAUGHTER OF THE INNOCENTS

After the Painting by Marco Benefial,
The Uffizi Gallery, Florence

I.

On the concrete seawall; rain and white-starred balloons
contrast black water, smiling stuffed elephants
and monkeys anchoring two thin strings, flowers

and a pinwheel just below them in the grass,
the only color in the frame near the clouds like fire
in the background, enveloping as if to shroud

the water below it, entomb it for our lifetime.
Oh my God, I made a mistake, I made a mistake, she rasped
as the black minivan entered the water and sank

slowly enough for her oldest son to escape—
three babies buckled in the back, unaware of anything
but their inability to breathe. At ten, the boy was strong

enough to flee—before the windows wouldn't roll down—
and swim through forty-degree water to safety, unable
to see through the black surrounding his eyes.

I'm sorry. You have to forgive me, she said to a relative
an hour before, not waiting for an answer—
click of the talk button before disconnection

and dial tone, the mother-of-four gripping the phone,
not yet realizing she would soon say to her children:
If I'm going to die, you're dying with me.

II.

In the painting, the woman—whose baby's face
is nearly half off the canvas, looking directly
into our eyes—closes in on the man's groin with a knife

29

poised to kill whatever it strikes. She holds
forcefully, arms wrapped so tightly around the torso
of her daughter that she almost strangles her

as the man's left hand pulls down her clothes—chest
and stomach exposed—breaths and screamed pleas escaping
the woman's lips: a meaning we'll never know. All around:

newborns in the midst of dying. While another woman,
to the left, hands folded, either pounds her son's stomach
or prays with curled fingers. A bluish-grey, the child already

looks like a ghost, so it must be prayer: a prayer that she
will die with her son. The innocents thrash and fight
as well as they can, without weapons, wrapped

around their children, caught in this moment, a moment
the men in the distant background, on a balcony,
cannot see or simply ignore, while in a matter of minutes

blood will spill, black clouds will slide across the sky,
and the steps will be torn down years later: remains
in ruins, years of rain erasing wounds we'll never feel.

Two

SEEING GEORGE SODINI
IN A RED FORD F-150 ON I-88 EAST

It has to be him: white mustache, cold eyes, plans running

      through his brain. When I look over, as he stares unblinking,

I want to tell you it's him, your eyes still scanning the road, fingers

        twisting through curls, mouthing words to some awful song

on a station wrestling with static. He didn't drive a red Ford

      but he's in one now, almost a year after he went into LA Fitness,

turned off the lights, and started shooting: over fifty rounds

      and only four people dead. Because three women died

we can't call it fortuity, but at some point we must—

      he was too afraid to do it with the lights on. *Maybe soon,*

he wrote, *I will see God and Jesus*, most likely believing

      his every word. And we have to imagine the last shred

of light he saw—women in their workout clothes, mothers

      and daughters, married and divorced—flipping the switch

in that open space, seeing nothing but each shot's white flash

      before he put the gun to his temple. Sometimes I can't help

but imagine you there: a slug piercing your thigh, heartbeat quickened

      or slowed to an immeasurable pulse. But you weren't there.

We had just been married. And planned the move to start

      our new life, one always ruined by my thoughts: your body

on the elliptical down the road at the gym, and the world's

      sick joke that includes us both, when it happens again as I wait

for the sirens to grow deafening, his eyes to turn away from mine.

THROUGH THE WINDOW

Through the window, I couldn't tell if she was beautiful:
a girl three stories below on the corner of our street,
maybe 19, her voice tearing off the sidewalks, cell phone

glued to her ear. I strained to listen from the balcony,
heard the phrases *Go to hell* and *I have no more pills*

between her crying. At almost 2:30—the bars
closed, most families asleep, and Jess gone
to bed hours ago—I opened the fridge, grabbed a can

of Miller Lite for the girl, drunk enough not to care
what happened, wanting to see if she was, in fact, beautiful.

I would be valiant: see if she needed cash for a cab,
avoid a kiss if she reached out in desperation or revenge.
But her voice woke someone, maybe a family, and left

two cop cars and an ambulance surrounding her. I watched
the soundless lights turn her hair from red to blond to blue

as cold aluminum numbed my palm. No cars passed.
She answered questions I couldn't understand, four cops
swarming her. Then her pleas: she would go to a friend's,

not cause a disturbance. Soon, the stretcher before her,
three of them it took to lift her on, tie the restraints.

Still her crying, howling, before a punch to her chest.
I dropped the can. Another punch to her chest. One of them
cupped his hand over her mouth as they rolled her

into the ambulance. I watched as it drove off, each cop
slowly entering his vehicle, the lights fading to black.

INEXCUSABLE APOLOGIA

Too late to think about tomorrow, I do it anyway.
　　And while I'll still be sleeping, your drive on I-95
　　　　I always imagine, every situation different. First,

a man in a car with a siren, flickering and silent,
　　wearing away its dark black paint. He stops, tells you
　　　　to get out. Since there's a passenger in your rearview,

you do. Mimicking the original *Vanishing*, he wraps a cloth
　　around your mouth, but I can't describe your struggle.
　　　　Car abandoned. People passing see nothing. Excuses:

they were also on their way to work. Then the only day
　　of snow: your blown tire, a piercing nail, skidding
　　　　into the right lane as your breathing finally slows.

A man wearing trustworthy clothes—a business suit,
　　a wedding ring—offers to drive you to the nearest mechanic.
　　　　There cannot be a cell phone anywhere.

This time, in *Breakdown*, Jeff Taylor will not save his wife.
　　Then the scene in *Fargo*: you the passenger, someone else
　　　　driving, where Grimsrud, eyeing you helpless

and broken-legged, shoots you off camera, ending
　　in quick flash and gone-before-you-know-it powder burns.
　　　　You asked me once, like it was some kind of game,

to change something about you. I would answer this:
　　you trust too much. Everyone around you, and even I,
　　　　can make choices for you, and believe me, I often wonder

if some stranger will make them for you too: gun to your head,
　　chemical cocktail wrapped too tight, the way
　　　　you writhe, the call I get too many hours later.

35

COUNTDOWN

"So much we have to trust..."
                    - Tomas Tranströmer

It's not that I dream of such hands touching God. It's easy, I know,
            to believe anything
can kill us. Popcorn causes cancer. Saccharine burrows holes

            in our skin, burning
like track marks up and down our arms. But it's not enough to believe
            in love. The rocks

are shifting beneath the undertow, waiting to take us with them.
            The railings are too short,
and we may plummet in our dreams. If we wake, let us see ourselves

            in this hospital
without light, without windows, too far from home. And if someone
            should ask us

how we got here, let us answer by walking under the stars—
            our steps echoing
in the hallways of our lives, ending with this bridge, what lies beneath:

            addicts who won't
bother us while our teeth clench the tourniquet, while we plunge
            underneath the night sky.

POINTED LIKE A GUN TOWARD YOUR CHEST

That a vest could be placed between sternum
      and hands, between wrist and gunmetal, lessening
the blow from the first rip of skin, but with it
      comes the vision of everything as slowly
as possible: your mouth agape slower, your breath

      in before out and slower, the bark of your terrier
slower, and because of the echo, even louder,
      your previously unshattered wrist slower
to the whole inside of your heart. Or that it's night
      and you can see nothing in the first place, only

when the few cars pass, the curtains hiding slightly
      the streaked yellow turned every color but black,
as the black then turns to blinding, and really you
      are watching this happen, some murder, or is it
a suicide, taking place at the building across

      the street, the eighth-floor window in the complex
where you noticed the woman, then noticed
      again her boyfriend, saw their mouths twisted
and ravaged, his hands in the air, her hands
      covering her heart, and the dog barking, but you

couldn't hear a sound, not even the bullet through
      her chest as you watched his shadow trampling
down the stairs from the fluorescent lights above each
      stairwell, hoping this was on television, a late night
silent short film on some distorted channel, the man

      walking quickly out the main door, and that the hero
saved the girl, called 911, belting breathlessly scene-
      after-scene without skipping a beat. That it wasn't
on the news the next morning. That it didn't take an hour
      for the ambulance to arrive. That the director appeared

from behind mirrors and sheets, and she got up
    finally, smiling, her exaltation letting you know
the scene was perfect, the execution divine, that she
    would do it again if needed, if the light wasn't right,
if her fear wasn't palpable, if they needed more blood.

Variation on a Landscape

After Stephen Roach's Photograph, *Ajar*

It begins with feigned invitation: preventing drunk driving,
choking her because she had a knife, about to slit her wrists
or yours. Always the excuse of opening: disorientation

and busted locks, black rooms and broken windows as if
we can go anywhere without warning, raid unfinished duplexes
to plunge into veins, climb house frames in blackened ash

to find clues how the families died. Or an excuse to enter
the neighbor's back door, where she was *always naked, posing
like some goddess.* Headlines composed of longing, testimonies

and court breakdowns, maps of entry and escape routes.
Always some house on a tree-lined street. Always some neighbor.
The bail and house arrest. Always repeating less than one year later.

Finding Ray's Sausage in East Cleveland on Google Earth

...identified in press reports as The Cleveland Strangler

Lucky gave me the idea to search for aerial photographs
of Alice Sebold's path post-rape—from a friend's house, through
the Thornden Park Amphitheatre—before she reached her dorm.

I could read no more after zooming to each location.
Days later: news of Anthony Sowell, who requested help in prison
and got nothing before the almost-snuff-film reports, his bi-polar

rapes and abuse. The stories that followed seemed unreal: coercion
with King Cobra malt liquor, unknown smells from his house
next door to Ray's Sausage, while the cops ignored every call for years.

Finally, after one woman's report, the cops entered, found eleven
bodies in crawlspaces, under the porch, skull in a bucket
on the third floor. Anthologies exist of artifacts: sad clowns painted

by Gacy, Fish's letter to Gracie Budd's parents, and the horned, cartoon
demons of Richard Ramirez. But what will remain of Sowell
in the future? Talks of the wrong side of town, racism, the constant

beating of women? Now I can't stop: aerial views from films,
headlines of tragedies, property lines and their clusters of houses—
as if we could tear off roofs with our hands, never able to look inside.

HOW SHE WAS FOUND

Virginia Commonwealth University, 2005

We forget grey photos of the farmhouse, one of many
crumbling, simply existing faintly in Virginia backwoods:
unmown and untouched fields, grass and its photographic

wavering among dry wind, before the blue-hooded sweatshirt
was eventually found an hour from Richmond, from the dorms
towering in their cluster downtown, among other buildings

erected over gravesites of slaves, etiolated bones we never knew
were buried beneath poured coffee, the slow glug of water coolers,
pressed pinstripes, cubicles like honeycombs, immaculate

in their blank uniformity and infinite sameness. The remains
were connected to her from the color and hood, the last
outfit she wore, sliding by delayed, already wraithlike

in the black-and-white glow of the security camera, the video shown
over and over on every news station: AMBER Alert signs
plastering telephone poles, corroding in piles in Cary Street bars.

And Ben Fawley's apartment on Mulberry where he went
after he strangled her, after he pushed her into high grass,
moved her car, panicking before the inevitable calm,

before talking to himself near the window unit's drip and drone.
I never found out which one of us was her freshman
composition teacher that year—maybe they couldn't

reveal it. In the end, what I want to know is how many days
it took before he forgave himself, lived in the fading caul
of his regret like a passenger in a plane going down, nothing

to look for amid the sea of blue seats, unable to catch his breath
in that swarm of two hundred pairs of closed eyes, the sky
refracting its million angles of light and prayer and endlessness.

BURNING BUILDING

This city is ours, you said, hair blowing like invisible seeds
dying at separation from the root. We both knew then
how true you meant to be. But we owned nothing, not even

love the way we saw it then, wavering in colder nights
like ghosts passing through our lives. Even they had given up.
And looking at you now, I can't say exactly the bad choices

I'll make, but I know there will be many. They'll exist
like our words crystallized into our former selves
when we focused on nothing, never escaped the chill inside

our bodies, near the fireplace we never touched, for fear
of burning the building to its core. But I would concentrate
on your eyes then, white flames licking beams to blackness,

and would hold you until the lights swirled miles away,
speeding at us like it mattered: if we were sleeping, drunk,
too in love to admit our lives would soon be too much.

Lost then and now, I can see how in love I was with it all:
your hand warm in mine, the many car accidents we saw
at the corner of the one-way street. And our entwining, eyes

closing as sirens slalomed and tore off walls, fading like our breath
upon the coldest day in history. When our sleep
was the sleep of the gods. We never woke that way again.

SIX BLOCKS AWAY

Truly I haven't measured the distance:
> our whole city in grids and houses burning
>> late into the night, black tread marks still left

on her body in the morning. Female,
> twenty years old: some domestic dispute
>> near apartments we drive by every single day.

But what's to be said that hasn't already?
> You don't set foot in Gilpin Court unless
>> you're buying drugs, but here—the museums

spilling their histories like blood—we never
> expect a thing. And there are times when the sun,
>> as it rises, leads us to believe in something

hopeful or sacred while the crows begin
> their cawing, letting us know that someone
>> will soon light a fire to everything we love.

Delay: Richmond International Airport

At first I'm too tired to drive, the last calls
already ten minutes past, blanketing snow
floating down from the darkness

to evaporate on roads or form
black ice, their veiled patches predicting
how many cars sliding, hearts stopped,

guard rails twisted like silly putty
the next morning. I have to pick up our friend
after the first plane's cabin pressure was too low

and everyone thought it was the end.
Steering past the mottled glow
of Capital One offices flickering like teeth

in some dark mouth, I imagine what goes on
inside: affairs and imminent broken
marriages, funneled money and future jail time.

Is everyone in such clear thought at this hour?
Through these winding curves there's a stillness
of indescribable beauty. Yet in Los Angeles

another father murdered his entire family
with seven bullets to their heads. I told myself
I wouldn't think about it: the mind of a five-year-old

as his father presses cold steel to his temple.
Past the blaze of gas stations and failing
motels—their lots empty aside from a few stragglers

lost in this fading morning—I see Jen's plane
coasting under the few clouds left, thick stars
I lose track of as I follow. The airport lights never

turn off in this place where we all end up
someday. I can't predict how I'll die,
but mostly I imagine a puddle jumper dive-bombing

into an ocean with no miracle in sight. Finally
I park, no one else there, my steps echoing
        like timpanis off the concrete of arrivals, departures.

        Everything empty now. Then the few
with bags in hand waiting for someone's return.
        Near 3 a.m. we're both on cell phones, wondering

        where the other may be. And when I see her
walking toward me, I hope the snow never turns to ice
        that we'll never owe a thing to this nightlong world.

WATCHING *GHOST* AT THE RITZ-CARLTON

Finally, the silence. The workers on the east and west wings
        have ceased their drilling and now just the wind through

everything it can touch. It would be torturous to walk
        through life like this: yearning for cigarettes or lips, undressing

in front of everyone with no one who can see. We don't belong
        among doctors and deep southern accents, the overcast sky

above ashen water the color of a body pulled from a hundred
        yards out. The dead can't feel water, there's no riptide alert—

sharks sensing blood from razor cuts, the fear of drowning.
        But there can be no relief. All of them look like ghosts: floating

through long hallways, cell phones glued to their ears, wrapped
        in thousand-dollar suits, alligator purses under their arms.

Since jumping into bodies can't happen, we hope we've done
        enough to stay here, avoid shadows from darkened street lamps

stretched into formless beings to drag us somewhere under
        this earth, our penance we believed in afforded no longer.

Meth Mouth and Last Rites

We saw them more and more with soiled blankets, empty milk cartons
      and cigarette butts, moth-ridden coats and mismatched shoes.
Then they came from alleys, boarded warehouses, empty jails
      and tennis courts, where they were living all along. And the smiles:
lye and red sulfur, ammonia and lithium, candy bars and Coke.
      They weren't meaning to harm. But then the curious fathers,
mothers in parked vans near the high school, inhaling in groups,
      windows painted black. The children younger and younger:
those who stole cars before they hid the keys, ditched them
      in sinkholes or quarries. Soon everyone was walking, smiles
turned into their mouths. There were rumors that no one wanted
      to be identified—the enamel worn and gone, no pulling
or drilling, just slow molder to black—or that someone had
      a photographic memory, could teach others of the world
now known to all. They never tried to come inside. Never rattled locks
      or broke front-door windows. Never threw bombs or Molotovs
through second floors. But no one came out of their homes. Tenants
      in third-floor apartments watched from balconies: stolen bikes
and Radio Flyers, nothing motorized. They needed each alchemic rush
      and got faster as days moved on. They gathered more, culled
from sheds, built crude cars from wrenched wheels and nails.
      We communicated with others across streets, wrote huge letters
on paper spelling words and basic sentences. We had distant laughs
      before setbacks over planning. Someone had to go out and see.
Someone had to enter that world. But there were never volunteers.

BACKGROUND

Near dusk, the sky's turned a smudged orange thumbprint
over the horizon, and with the TV volume blasted
and door locked, what I first think about is someone else

with me—some affair ten states away, when our love
has irrevocably faded—but we're alone, watching the news
of a middle-schooler who took a bullet to the head

on a playground, his mother pleading to God. Then a family
turned to ashes from circuit sparks, dry rotting wood, flames
blazing until morning. And the series of carjacks becoming

as much as one every few days, all from the voice of a newscaster
whose name we won't remember. Deception's all around us—
the waves now roiling under black sky—and when we finish,

bad news turned finally to sports, the sound now to mute,
there is nothing to listen to but every shred of memory,
piercing us like brands pressed against our eyes.

HONEYMOON MEDITATION:
TSUNAMI EVACUATION PLAN

Occidental Grand Hotel, Punta Cana

This is all for nothing: high tide over the sand,
　　　　resort beaches spreading over a mile along the edge
of this island as I joke about what a tsunami
　　　　would look like, that it would appear as a dream
always instead of some reality. The myriad
　　　　disaster films: Hokusai's waves curling, white foam
swallowing the horizon line until the crash
　　　　of be-all-end-all, of crushing, endless water.
I picture us watching it from our balcony.
　　　　As it surges, I think *stucco* and wonder if that
makes up the roof, if I'll have enough strength
　　　　to push you to the top. You would balance
on my hands and pull yourself up like you've never
　　　　pulled before. There would be a lightning rod
rooted in the middle of the roof, and you
　　　　would wrap your limbs around it while your lungs
exhaled, concentrating calmly against
　　　　the impact. If together, I'd choose to die
knowing you have a chance, that God has
　　　　nothing to do with how tight you hold on.

STARGAZING

We're all accustomed to the stars, their luminescence
too far above our heads. Yet few know the names
or care to know because we're jealous of their lives

and deaths, always becoming something else, reborn
in the uncharted spaces we gaze into before our own
lives expire for good. And I wonder if those

who drown turn into angels, those taken by accident
instead of murder, who cared about their future lives
amidst the black pond's invisible circumference, almost

taunting, some long bony forefinger reaching out to take
what it deserves. But how do we find out about LifeHammers
and ResQMe Keychains if it isn't through tragedy? Practical

are de-icers for locks, a Maglite's thin beam gleaming
toward what we've lost. But *water enters the cabin like a flood*,
first in drips and slow percolation before it bursts the cracks

like black holes, the gush and fill too quick to stop. How
do we practice before it happens? *Relax. Conserve your energy
and air.* Would you rather be burned alive or freeze to death?

What happens fastest? *If you sit and fight the whole way, you drown.*
Perseids. Quadrans Muralis. Beautiful names meaning nothing
in the end. *Stay as calm as possible.* They were speaking

of things we'll never know. *Keep your seatbelt on.* The sheriff
wanted to say they had trespassed. *Don't wait for the pressure
to equalize.* Who was driving? *Roll down or break the window.*

The collie couldn't imagine what was happening, its fur
swaying like seaweed. *Escape through a door.* There were
signals from a nearby tower: words of panic, static, before

cell phones floated away from their hands. *Look for bubbles
and follow the direction they're going.* In cars we're always afraid
of collision. There were Crash Test Dummies toys: clicked-in

plastic test center, two front-seat figures, multiple crash zones.
We got further from the walls each time, measured how far
their bodies would fly, broken pieces that weren't meant

to break. Everyone asks who's to blame. Were the headlights
turned on? Was there a drop-off into the dark they didn't see?
And does it matter? All we're left with is the last: *Swim to safety.*

VARIATION ON A LANDSCAPE

After William Eggleston's Photograph,
Downtown Morton, Mississippi

Let us have this atmosphere, the otherworldly pink clouds
        seconds away from careening to black, all of it glowing

in this Technicolor world. The lone streetlight, illuminating
        something we're both supposed to see, bleeds fluorescence

onto the Mustang, parked for days, abandoned
        in this lot among strip malls erected between miles

and miles of roads taking passengers somewhere
        they'll regret: an affair in Forkville, newborn in a trashcan

in Clifton, a father in Midway, car still running in his closed garage.
        What looks like a radio tower hovers above the building

to the left, the only one with a light on. I like to think of us
        in that room—smoking cheap cigarettes in black

and white, glaring out the window—thinking it's beautiful,
        that somehow we're never able to get things right.

ON THE MISSING FRENCH JET TWO DAYS BEFORE MY MOTHER LEAVES FOR PARIS

I met with a mother who lost her son, a fiancée who lost her future husband. I told them the truth.
          - French President Nicolas Sarkozy

And so again we're left with speculation: fortuity, accident, destiny.
The mouth makes its sounds, words forming quickly
into horror or love while lightning in the sky, if you're a passenger,

can't be described because those moments are always
your last. It's 3 a.m. Monday morning. Jess keeps waking from patients
calling for codeine cough syrup and hydrocodone

while the car alarm outside our window squalls like a fire truck
racing to save a million-dollar home in Chesdin Landing.
We've seen the darkness and CGI: feigned, blacked-out windows,

post-production lightning, but no one has lived to tell us
what the face of God looks like in the spiraling black, in the second
before the brain switches off like a light. What if

my mother had been on that flight? The London subway bombings,
9/11 bumps and cancellations, snipers on the freeways:
when *choice* becomes a made-up word. I like to imagine love letters

Neruda could compose, floating around like particle matter
in the crowd of passengers, all of them in a run-down theater
somewhere in a small town, laughing, holding hands

in some kind of celebration while the black screen scrolls slowly
the names in their futures, before all are revealed
in tomorrow's paper, ending as the projector finally cuts off.

Scream Fire

Everywhere elevators struggle to open, everywhere someone watches
        unequivocally, undressing
with his eyes: suit jacket or jeans, small knife or pistol hidden in a pocket
        under ill-fitting and cheap
fabric, so the eyes of the watching imagine back at him. Everywhere
        doors open, and each

pneumatic slam skips the heart, each handle metal-inside-metal,
        and the walking goes:
saunter, speed, mission, inside buildings ghosts walk through,
        unendangered, trapped
in this place where it all happened: unsuspecting hit, heart seizing up
        in a corridor, windows shut

to soundlessness, or the man who's had eyes on someone else, for years,
        amidst planning, following
her schedule, the patterns on each dress, and how she leaves sometimes
        from the fire escape
when she's running late on Fridays. Scream *fire*. What we tell little girls
        and boys about trouble,

about being followed, about never taking anything if you don't know
        the smooth touch
of their hand, the relative kindness in their voice, or when the hair hangs
        just over the eyes, eclipsing
the color, movement, how they can stare at you without your knowing.
        Scream *fire*, and someone,

love, will come running. They'll wield a hose, a gun, trained fists, words
        to talk someone down,
and someone will rush the doors, blood pumping through his veins.
        In this world, you will
tell them: *If you're to be saved, you'll be saved*. There's nothing
        that can stop the plans

God, in this life, has drawn for you. You tell them, every day, about
        all of this: the stories,
repetitive words to digest, devour, like blood-red paint on this palette

that will define your life,
rules you'll learn that can save you in any situation. As in there is no man
      at the corner store

who watches you from his tinted windows, exhaust spreading
      from a muffler never fixed,
caustically billowing in the coldest winter anyone's ever known.
      Scream *fire*. As in the clerk
will come running after you, the last words he hears not words,
      but a muffled choking

he'll remember all his life, after testimonies to the police, the pen's ink
      scratched into the pad
because the officer did not have another working. He'll remember
      the darkness with his hands
over his eyes, how he didn't see anything but jeans and a thick, slicked
      sheen of jet-black hair,

a license plate with numbers formed into incalculable equations
      of *What else could I have done?*
Scream *fire*, love, and the world will come to rescue you no matter what.
      Scream *fire*, and you will
exit unscathed, fall in love, live out your days among us all, and escape
      before you ever know the meaning.

Of This World

Until now, I've understood little of this world:
        the wavering and pitched music of a child's crying
                then reprieve, a carrying *Hello down there* from twenty

floors above. Below, somewhere, a woman sounds
        beautiful, her voice like an aria piercing off the east
                and west wings, almost as if she's afraid. It's Italian

I think, a language I can't speak and will never know.
        Someone shakes a soda can below: a toddler, his sister
                exclaiming when the can explodes, discovering

carbonation shatters the air like stars. In that
        unknowable distance, massive cruise ships are filled
                with forthcoming and supposed unsolved mysteries,

false love, and we wait and are satisfied with the bold,
        read words. Alcohol. Divorces. Our vices designed
                by headlines and our own uncaring for our lives.

We wait. Always for something better to happen.
        That inevitable decline and the hope, longing,
                the middle ground our bloated body, with all

its honesty intact, washed up on shore—
        the few midnight stars shining down, leaving
                one sliver of light we'll fade with in the end.

MUST READ AFTER MY DEATH

Dear voyeurism: I have never understood
what you've left in so many forms

as if you're some divine being and humans
you've left behind, for all of us to take in

as we wish. Dear Douglas Sirk: what you
showed us in the 50s—candy-colored sets

and Rock Hudson's lie—was so unspeakable then,
but it can't compare to how our lives play out now.

Dear oblivion: why have you left so many families
murdered at the hands of our fathers?

Why the random doors busted down, tape stretched
over mouths, fear that can never be palpable

on celluloid? Dear steamships floating
under the waterway bridge: where have

the controllers blown their ashes to the sea?
What happened then to the woman on the sand,

still in your mind as you watched her
from such a distance? *These are just conversations*

back and forth as if we were talking on the phone.
They're only valuable for the impact and effect they have

when you listen to them. Love: let us deny everything
as we stare into what we can never predict—

when the wood splinters and the frame burns
to the blackest of the earth's core.

NOTES—

"Delay: Dulles International Airport" – Italics reference lyrics from the song "Red Plains" on the album, *The Way It Is*, by Bruce Hornsby and The Range.

"Beginning with the Fear of Drowning" – References the film *Interiors* (1978, directed by Woody Allen).

"Watching the Live Fort Hood Memorial at Aspen Dental" – References the film *Affliction* (1997, directed by Paul Schrader).

"Variation on a Landscape (Without the cars...)" – References the film *The Poseidon Adventure* (1972, directed by Ronald Neame).

"To the Muses" – In February, 2010, in Melbourne, Florida, three teenage girls were on a narrow bridge when they were hit and killed by an oncoming train.

"Dear Sickness" – Thomas Mortimer IV, the man accused of slaying his wife, mother-in-law, and two young children, allegedly left behind two notes taking credit for the quadruple homicide in June, 2010.

"Seeing George Sodini in a Red Ford F-150 on I-88 East" – On August 4, 2009, in an LA Fitness health club in Collier Township, a suburb of Pittsburgh, Pennsylvania, George Sodini killed three women and injured nine before he took his own life.

"Inexcusable Apologia" – References the films *The Vanishing* (1988, directed by George Sluizer), *Breakdown*, (1997, directed by Jonathan Mostow) and *Fargo* (1996, directed by the Coen Brothers).

"Finding Ray's Sausage in East Cleveland on Google Earth" – References the memoir *Lucky* (1999, Alice Sebold).

"How She Was Found" – In August 2005, Taylor Behl moved to Richmond, Virginia to attend Virginia Commonwealth University. Two weeks later, on Labor Day, September 5, 2005, Behl disappeared. Acting on a tip one month later, VCU police located her remains in a rural area in Mathews County, Virginia.

"Watching *Ghost* at the Ritz-Carlton" – References the film *Ghost* (1990, directed by Jerry Zucker)

"Stargazing" – In November, 2009, three college softball players were found dead after their sport utility vehicle went into a pond on a North Dakota farm during a stargazing trip.

"On the Missing French Jet Two Days Before My Mother Leaves for Paris" – On June 1st, 2009, Air France Flight 447, with 228 people on a flight to Paris, vanished over the Atlantic Ocean after flying into towering thunderstorms and sending an automated message that the electrical system had failed. All passengers aboard were killed.

"*Must Read After My Death*" – References the documentary film of the same name (2007, directed by Morgan Dews).

ACKNOWLEDGMENTS

The author wishes to thank the editors of the following journals, in which these poems previously appeared, sometimes in earlier versions:

American Poetry Journal: "Variation on a Landscape (It begins with...)"

Anti-: "Scream Fire," "Through the Cities as We Move Closer to Our Wedding," "Variation on a Landscape (Let us have...)"

Barn Owl Review: "Last Page: U.S. Airways Safety Information Card"

Belmont Story Review: "Slaughter of the Innocents"

Blackbird: "Finding Ray's Sausage in East Cleveland on Google Earth"

Blue Mesa Review: "What Follows"

Boxcar Poetry Review: "Beginning with the Fear of Drowning"

Cave Wall: "Open Windows," "Pointed Like a Gun Toward Your Chest"

Collagist: "Stargazing"

Center: "Variation on a Landscape (Without the cars...)"

Conte: "Watching *Ghost* at the Ritz-Carlton"

Copper Nickel: "Seeing George Sodini in a Red Ford F-150 on I-88 East"

Diode: "Come Home to Me," "Dear Sickness," "How She Was Found," "Variation on a Landscape (Former horror-film...)," "Watching the Live Fort Hood Memorial at Aspen Dental," "What This Means"

Front Porch: "Burning Building," "City's Edge"

Hollins Critic: "Wishing for a Nocturne Instead of an Elegy"

iO: A Journal of New American Poetry: "To the Muses"

Lake Effect: "Countdown"

Linebreak: "Snowstorm and Power Outage"

Madison Review: "Sirens and Wildfire"

Nimrod: "Next Room"

Passages North: "Meth Mouth and Last Rites"

Pebble Lake Review: "Honeymoon Meditation: Flight Number 1967"

Phoebe: "Honeymoon Meditation: Tsunami Evacuation Plan," "*Must Read
    After My Death*" "Six Blocks Away"

Portland Review: "Delay: Richmond International Airport," "Variation on
    a Landscape (All these urban...)"

Tusculum Review: "Delay: Dulles International Airport"

Waccamaw: "Through the Window"

Whiskey Island Magazine: "Background," "Of This World"

420pus: "Inexcusable Apologia," "Last Words," "On the Missing French Jet
    Two Days Before My Mother Leaves for Paris"

*

Thank you to Kyle McCord, Nick Courtright, Corey Spaley, Nicholas
Reading, Sean Harris, Craig Beaven, Anna Journey, Joshua Poteat, Jon
Pineda, David Wojahn, Maria Mazzioti Gillan, and Joe Weil.

With gratitude to Binghamton University and the Marion Clayton Link
Fellowship in Creative Writing, which allowed me the time to finish this
book.

Finally, I'm eternally grateful for the sage advice of Gary McDowell and
Andrew McFadyen-Ketchum, who were both integral in helping me in so
many ways with these poems.

ABOUT GOLD WAKE PRESS

Gold Wake Press, an independent publisher, is curated by Nick Courtright and Kyle McCord. All Gold Wake titles are available at amazon.com, barnesandnoble.com, and via order from your local bookstore. Learn more at goldwake.com.

Available Titles:

Kelly Magee's *The Neighborhood*

Kyle Flak's *I Am Sorry for Everything in the Whole Entire Universe*

David Wojciechowski's *Dreams I Never Told You & Letters I Never Sent*

Mary Quade's *Local Extinctions*

Adam Crittenden's *Blood Eagle*

Joshua Butts' *New to the Lost Coast*

Mary Buchinger Bodwell's *Aerialist*

Becca J. R. Lachman's *Other Acreage*

Lesley Jenike's *Holy Island*

Tasha Cotter's *Some Churches*

Nick Courtright's *Let There Be Light*

Kyle McCord's *You Are Indeed an Elk, But This is Not the Forest You Were
        Born to Graze*

Hannah Stephenson's *In the Kettle, the Shriek*

Kathleen Rooney's *Robinson Alone*

Erin Elizabeth Smith's *The Naming of Strays*

ABOUT KEITH MONTESANO

Keith Montesano is the author of *Housefire Elegies* (Gold Wake Press, 2017), *Scoring the Silent Film* (Dream Horse Press, 2013), and *Ghost Lights* (Dream Horse Press, 2010). He recently earned his PhD in English and creative writing at Binghamton University, and currently works as an editor and writer in Pittsburgh, Pennsylvania, where he lives with his family.

CPSIA information can be obtained
at www.ICGtesting.com
Printed in the USA
FFOW02n1949221216
30572FF